ECHOES OF HEAVEN

OLAMIDE OTI-AKAPPO

A POETRY COLLECTION

Insightful words, inspired imaginations
www.householderbooks.com

Echoes of Heaven
Copyright © 2023 by Olamide Oti-Akappo

Published in 2023 by Householder Books. All rights reserved. No part of this publication may be reproduced, stored in a retrieval system or transmitted in any form or by any means electronic, mechanical, photocopying, recording or otherwise without the prior permission of the publisher.

Scripture quotations marked (NLT) are taken from the Holy Bible, New Living Translation, copyright ©1996, 2004, 2015 by Tyndale House Foundation. Used by permission of Tyndale House Publishers, Carol Stream, Illinois 60188. All rights reserved.

Edited by Anthony Okpunor
Book Design and Illustrations by Toluwanimi Babarinde
Book Design Copyright © 2023 by Householder Books
Send inquiries to hello@householderpublishing.com

Print ISBN: 978-1-0878-6507-2
E-book ISBN: 978-1-0878-8118-8
Published in the United States of America
Printed by the IngramSpark global distribution network.

Library of Congress Control Number: 2023932010

I dedicate this book to God.
Thank You Abba for loving me so
well, and for writing this book with
me. I love You because You first
loved me.

PART ONE - Page 7

Of Longings and God-sized Voids, 2020
To the Weary Traveller, 2018
More Than the Joy of Fulfilled Promises, 2018
Love Waits, 2018
Here and Now, 2019

PART TWO - Page 15

Dear Broken-hearted One, 2018
Hope, 2018
Prisoner of Hope, 2020
To my Father's Antsy Daughters, 2018
Intimacy with God, 2020

PART THREE - Page 25

Beauty for Ashes, 2017
The Past, 2018
On Thoughts, 2020
Finding Wonder, 2020
Beyond the Veil, 2018

PART FOUR - Page 33

Dear Child, 2015
Come Home, 2018
For Abba, 2017
Heartstrings, 2016
She knows Who She Is, 2018

PART FIVE - Page 45

Worry, 2020
Mountains and Valleys, 2018
Refuge, 2016
Rest, 2019
The Brevity of Life, 2020

PART SIX - Page 53

Some Days, 2018
Conversations with My Father, 2015
Audience of One, 2019
Jar of Clay, 2021
A Psalm, 2015

PART SEVEN - Page 63

Looking Ahead, 2013
Love Garden, 2019

PART EIGHT - Page 69

Light Be, 2019
This is War, 2020
The King of the Jews, 2020
The Rising, 2015

PART NINE - Page 75

A Nation Bleeds, 2020
Mama's Hope, 2015
National Awakening, 2020
One Day Soon, 2016

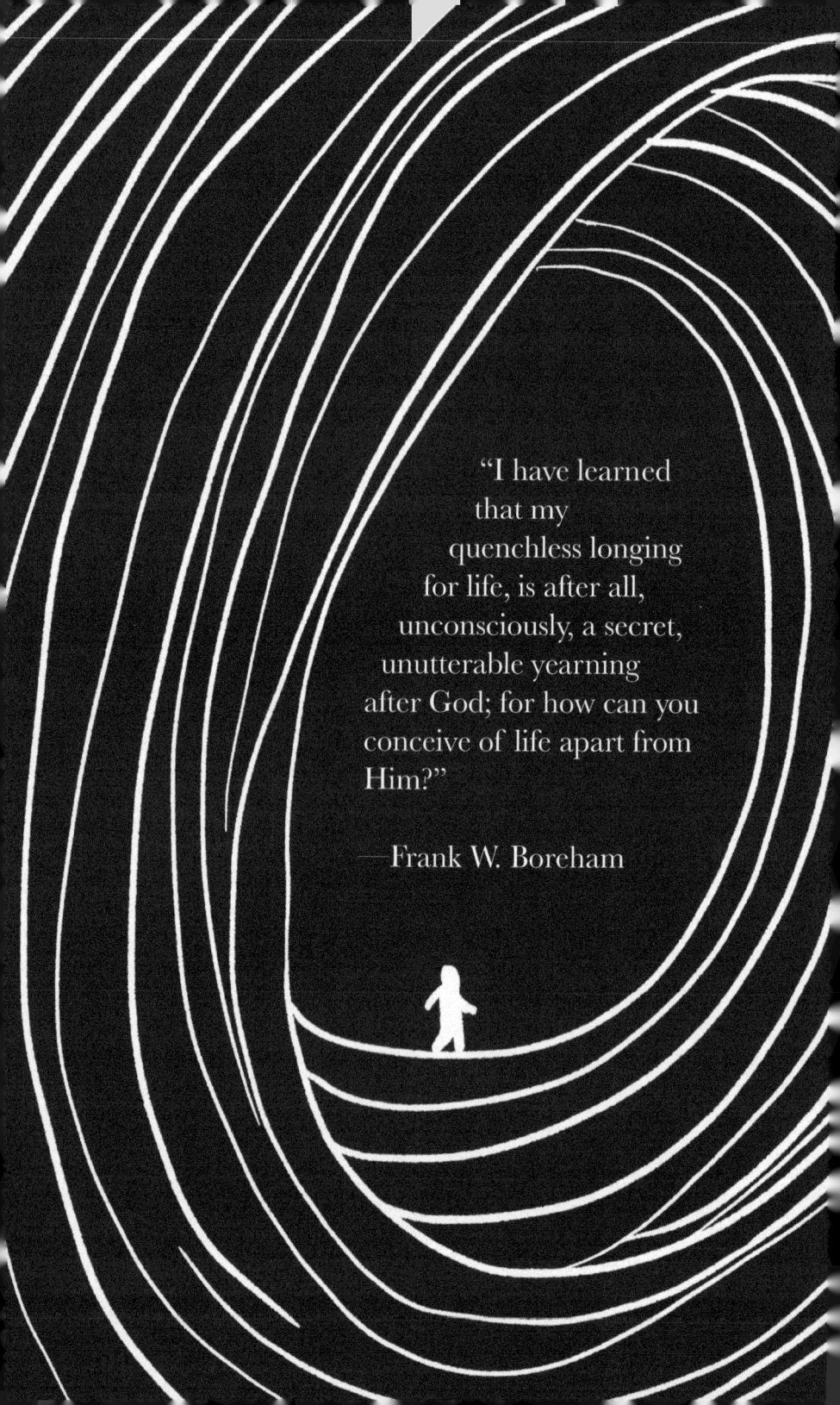

"I have learned that my quenchless longing for life, is after all, unconsciously, a secret, unutterable yearning after God; for how can you conceive of life apart from Him?"

—Frank W. Boreham

part one

OF LONGINGS AND GOD-SIZED VOIDS

This longing,
This inexplicable thirst that won't go away
Is your Saviour's call to deeper.

The fleeting romance with the Word,
The hurried prayers before the day begins
Can no longer suffice.

Your heart knows,
Everything in you knows,
Nothing else will ever be enough.

It's time to go deeper,
There's so much to know.

AND SO LITTLE TIME...

TO THE WEARY TRAVELLER

Your dusty boots tell a tale,
Of dusty paths and muddy roads.
As you stand at the crossroads,
The war in your mind rages on.

Dare to ask the One who calls you His own,
The answer may tarry, but it will come.
And like fog lifting off a harmattan morning,

His light will flood your eyes.

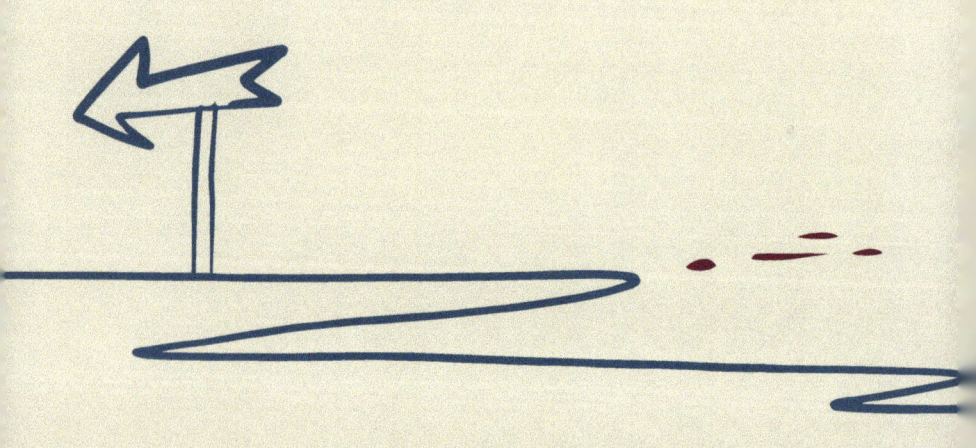

MORE THAN THE JOY OF FULFILLED PROMISES...

is the joy of seeing Jesus
face-to-face,
and knowing that
my hope and trust in Him
was not in vain.

In that moment,
there would be no questions,
No tears, no pain.

Just joy, greater than
anything I can ever imagine.

LOVE WAITS

In my darkest moments;
When I was knee-deep
in sin,
Oblivious to my fallen
state,
Your love chased me.

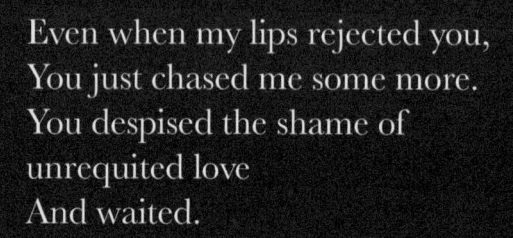

Even when my lips rejected you,
You just chased me some more.
You despised the shame of
unrequited love
And waited.

You knew the scales would fall.
You knew the pain of regret would
almost consume me.
That I would need new eyes and a
new heart.
You gave me You.

Like a little child,
May my eyes always light up with
wonder when You speak.

Ours is an eternal dance—
To a never-ending song.
You will never let go,
This is your eternal promise.

Even here, Even now.
Your love surrounds me as a cloak.

Even here, Where all that should be is emptiness—
Your life flows more abundantly.

I turned my face away from Yours,
Enthralled by the magnetic pull of the flesh.
As if it could satisfy the depth of my hungry soul.
I should have reaped in equal measure,
But for Your grace.

Even now, I'm soaked in love.
I'm drenched in grace.
I'm in awe of You, Lord,
And how much You love me.

If being a son could be earned,
Yours would not have been born.
If my rights as a son could be withdrawn,
then the Holy Spirit would never have come.

You pursue me so relentlessly
Like I'm the only one in the room.

Even here, Even now,
I'm experiencing Your love again.
Just like the first time,
Even better.

HERE AND NOW

"Earth's troubles fade in the light of heaven's hope."

—Billy Graham

part two

DEAR BROKEN-HEARTED ONE

Don't believe the lie that this will always be your story.
What better place to meet the Comforter than in the place of brokenness?
What better place to be delivered than in the valley of the shadow of death?

This is undeniably a part of your story, but it is not the whole story.
There is so much more,
God is writing for you—
A tale bigger than your imaginations,
A song louder than your fears,
Stay close,

Your God is more than enough.
Your God is more than enough.

HOPE

In the waiting,
She's changing.
She's enlarging
from the inside out.

And though it looks
like nothing is
happening,
She knows His hand is at
work.
Weaving a story never before read,
Painting a picture never before seen,
And though it looks like everything is the
same,
He is bringing new wine out of nothing.
Rebuilding what was broken beyond redemption,
His mouth is calling forth the future,
Soon it will all burst out in living colour.
She will stand in awe and be amazed,
As darkness gives way to light.

PRISONER OF

Who am I that He is mindful of me?
Why does my heart drum wildly in His presence?

Why do I hope for tomorrow even in the midst of a painful present,
And the distant echo of a sour past?
As though I were a prisoner chained to hope.

    Why bother to explain something that defies natural laws?

    Must everything be explained?
    My hope is a mystery.

I have found a hope
that transcends times and seasons.
I have found a hope
that cannot be taken away.

>Wrapped up in the person of the One
>who holds all the answers.
>Everyday, the world tries to latch on to it,
>
>Hoping to take it away and trample upon it,
>But the One who gave it, has already held on too tightly to me.
>
>If I were a prisoner,
>Let me be a prisoner of hope.

HOPE

Be patient,
Don't rush into
anything
prematurely.
In the waiting,
learn the ways of
Your Father.

TO MY FATHER'S
ANTSY DAUGHTERS

Teach your ears to know His voice.
Teach your feet to walk in His steps.
Teach your heart to love.

You will soon find that God is

MORE
THAN
ENOUGH

INTIMACY WITH GOD

We are changing,
No one stays the same.
But God never changes.
He is as Emmanuel now
as He was then.

Sometimes, I am more more
aware of Him,
But it doesn't change the fact
that He never leaves.
He is always there, peering into
the room and asking to come in.
Never forcing open the door even
though He could,
He is that gentle.

My heart knows what my mind
tries to deny sometimes,
I need Him.
I need Him more today than I
did yesterday.
I'll need Him more tomorrow
than I do today.
There's no point where all that I have
tasted will ever be enough.
I need Him.

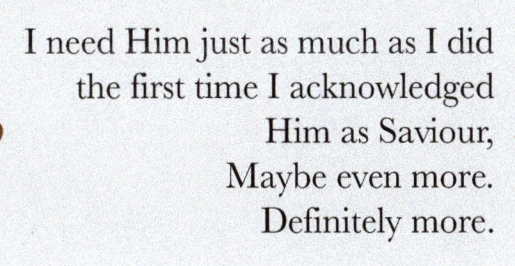

I need Him just as much as I did
the first time I acknowledged
Him as Saviour,
Maybe even more.
Definitely more.

There are no oars to rest on.
This is not a fishing expedition.
This is life, real life.

Let me be the one that points others to
Jesus,
But let that never be the true essence of my
life.
Let the true essence of my life be;
I have found a love greater than life itself.
It's the love of Jesus.
My Saviour and Friend.

And let this be enough,
More than anything else can ever be.
May I never be weary of seeking You first,
May my delight always be in finding you.

"This means that anyone who belongs to Christ has become a new person. The old life is gone; a new life has begun!

— 2 Corinthians 5:17 NLT

part three

The past cuddles up to me every night,
slipping ever so subtly beneath the sheets,
taking me on a road trip to memory lane.
I remember when...

I am great at remembering, you see.
She conjures up stories in which I am the villain
and she is the victim.
She has become my best friend.
I lay awake at night waiting for visits.

Last night she didn't
come,
Someone else was there.
He called Himself—Healer.
He took her and turned her into
something I don't even recognise.

BEAUTY FOR ASHES

She's no longer the old festering wound that
eats me up from the inside.
She's now beauty,
the scars Healer left are
too beautiful to describe.
I display them now for all to see.

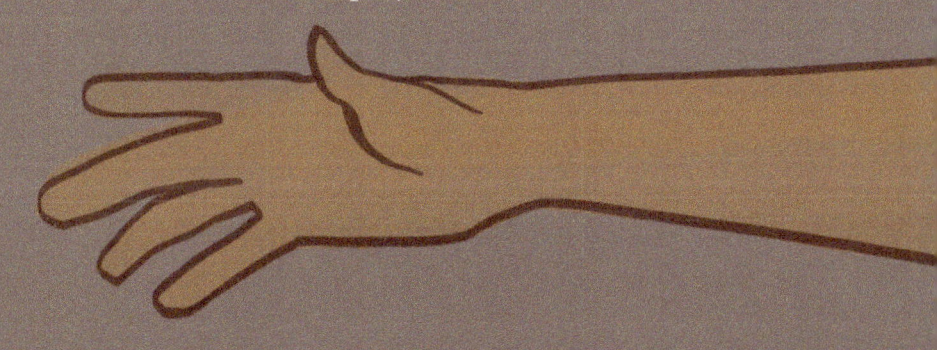

They are my trophies from war.
I wear them with dignity now.
The past? She no longer exists.
All I see now is beauty where ash once was.

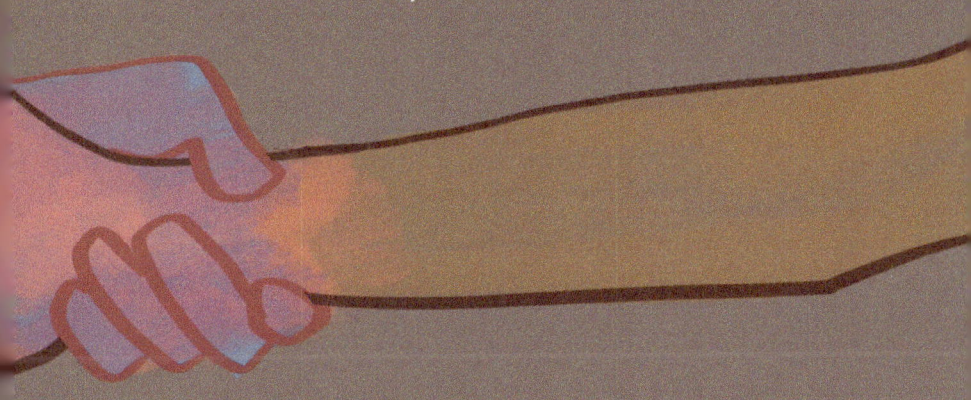

The past with all its trappings
came knocking yesterday.
Bitter-sweet nothings poured
in when I opened the door.

I gave it an inch,
it took a mile.

Dragging along with it regret, longing,
nostalgia:
3 foolish friends who often go
everywhere together,
luring willing victims in with a lie:
"The past was much better than
the present, perhaps even better
than the future (that has not existed
yet)."

A pillar of salt stands just outside
the gates of Sodom and Gomorrah.
A testament and a warning,
"Do not look back."
Or, "Look back at your own peril."

THE PAST

Yesterday, I shut the door
just as quickly as I opened it,
the past with all its trappings ran along,
dragging with it the 3 foolish friends.
At the booming sound of my,
"No, not today, not tomorrow, not ever."

Amen? Amen.

ON THOUGHTS

Hurry now, child.
Take those thoughts captive—
those lies that appear as truth,
running awry in your mind,
and putting chains on you that I fought to
remove.

Stand up child.
Declare the truth that you know,
and they'll go scurrying away like the cowards
that they are before you—son of God.

You know the truth,
say it and mean it.
And the light will break in,
where darkness dared to cast a shadow.
For who the Son sets free is free indeed.

FINDING WONDER

Every day we're alive, we leak wonder.
Like raindrops from the sky.
Little drops make a mighty ocean.

What used to amuse us no longer does.
The company we cherished now bore us.
The places we once loved to visit no longer excite us.

Once we were babes,
easily amused and entertained.
By the silly cooing of our parents,
awestruck that we could vocalise words like 'papa',
amazed that our feet could carry us when we took
that first step.

Now we seldom remember,
the falls and trips that got us here.

How does one recover wonder?
How does the ocean of wonder
become clouds again?
What happens when we let the
wonderful One in?

The One who never tires of us,
who always delights in us,
who loves us unconditionally.
We find it in Him.
He is the Wonder-full One.

To those who live behind the veil,
Whose eyes are darkened by ignorance,
Whose ears are deaf to His voice,
Whose hearts are made of stone;

There is life beyond the veil,
This is where hope lives.
Where fear flees,
Where death no longer kills.

BEYOND THE VEIL

Listen to the gentle tugging of
His hands on your heart,
Look! Light is demolishing your arguments,
His hands are creating in you a new heart,
Giving you Himself; Spirit without measure.

Hear the echoes of heaven,
Hear the songs of angels as they dance over you,
To the one who dares to find life beyond the veil,

WELOME HOME

"The ache for home lives in all of us, the safe place where we can go as we are and not be questioned."

—Maya Angelou

part four

DEAR CHILD

I LOVE YOU. I WISH YOU BELIEVED ME

Day after day, my heart breaks as you deny Me.
Thoughts of me make you cringe
as you question My existence,
I call to you, but you do not answer.
Your ears are shut to the sound of My voice.
Your heart cold as ice, unyielding as ever.

I knew you before you were formed,
I beamed at your conception,
I rejoiced at your birth.
I believed in you when no one else would,
Tended to your bruises,
Soothed your pain.

Listen, My heart beats for you.
Your name is tattooed on the palm of My hand,
Your face is etched forever in My memory.

I will not give up on you My child,
Look past your hurt, and see what can still be.
I never promised that your life would be perfect,
Roses have thorns too, you see.
If you would just trust in Me,
Then you will see,
That only I can give you peace.
I am your Father,
and I love you like no one else can.

COME HOME

You have been despised and rejected,
tossed to and fro by lies so perfect they sound
like the truth.
You have been told that no one has ever made it
out alive,
That this maze of lies will soon be your grave,
and hell would be your eternal home.
You cannot imagine a better place for you,
filthy, sinful you.

It would be another lie,
if you say you have never felt your heart stir,
and you have never heard His soft knock
He is here everyday,
knocking on the door of your heart,
asking for an invitation.

Your fate is not sealed yet,
your time has not run out.
Be brave, open the door to Truth.
Choose the life you were made to live.
Come over to the other side,
to Love and Light.

Come home, to Grace and Peace.
Come home.

FOR ABBA

My eyes strain to see the end from the beginning.
something only Yours were meant to do.
You watch as I go round in circles,
turning to everything and everyone except You,
trying to carry burdens my shoulders are too frail to bear.

Fear stares me in the face,
daring me to step out in faith,
certain of my downfall when you promised to catch me.
I say a resounding 'yes' to a life of reckless abandon,
like a child, I'll live on every word that proceeds from your mouth.
Obeying your every command.
Joyfully carrying out your instructions.

You are good,
darkness gives way to Your light.
You are powerful, all-knowing, intentional.

You are love.
My life is in your hands.
Your hands drip with provision.
Your mouth overflows with words of life.
I say a resounding 'yes' to this life of abundance.

You are everything I need.
You are the answer to all my questions
You fill in every void gracefully.
I say a resounding 'yes' to this life of peace,
as you still the storms raging within my heart.

HEARTSTRINGS

my mind is a hollow mess of
a thousand echoes
bouncing off the walls of my heart.
they whisper to me in loud voices,
preying on labile feelings and desires.

my gaze rests upon
glitters and sparkles.
with eyes like lust, I stare
coveting the things I cannot have,
and the days long gone.

this flesh made from clay
craves to be admired and adorned,
it needs trophies and applause—
it delights in vain glory.

like the strings of
a newly wound guitar,
you pluck gently yet firmly,
producing a melody so perfect it hurts.
you hold out Your hand for a dance,
my feet stay glued, tired from
the journey of mistakes past.

I hear the words
Your mouth need not speak,
"trust, put your hand in Mine, dance."
I see your eyes swim with tears,
your hand is still held out,
your body poised to dance with me.

you strip away gently
with hands like love,
the debris upon my heart,
breathing me to life.
you quiet my will firmly
with words like fire,
setting me ablaze,
breaking me to stillness.

SHE KNOWS WHO SHE IS

She knows whose she is,
Her heart delights in this knowledge.

The mouth of the LORD speaks for her.
His words are a balm for her heart.
Her shelter in a raging storm.

His light shines upon her path,
She walks in sync with His steps.

Harvest is springing up out of the wilderness.
A pathway is opening in the most unlikely places.
Once despised, now accepted.
Once lost, now found.
Once ashamed, now restored.

She is her Father's daughter,
An embodiment of love and grace.
His peace is the wind in her sails,
His word is her only anchor.

Though the storms come,
and the winds beat against
her boat,
God is in the midst of her;
A Strong and Mighty One.

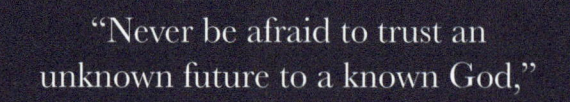

"Never be afraid to trust an unknown future to a known God,"

—Corrie Ten Boom

part five

WORRY

Why do you spend hours pondering over
things that you can't even change?
Time better spent worshipping,
or even sleeping.

Why mind, do you go round in circles?
scheming and planning,
trying to figure things out alone,
time better spent, resting.

Why feet, do you struggle so?
going everywhere but where you need to be,
hustling that won't get you anywhere.

FIND REST IN JESUS

author and Finisher
of your faith.
Giver of life and hope.

MOUNTAINS AND VALLEYS

Through the highs and lows,
mountains and valleys,
oceans and deserts
Christ is all that matters.
Though the promise may seem like
an echo in the wind,
too distant and out of your reach,
remember the One who promised.

He never fails.
Stop your striving.
Stay close to His heart.
Eyes fixed upon His face.
Learn His ways,
know His thoughts,
He makes all things beautiful.

And come what may,
remember that it's really all about Jesus.

REFUGE

As the tides rise,
And my fears with it,
My eyes search for the shore—
Looking wildly for arms
made with clay.

As the waves billow,
You test the limits of my trust,
And ask me to come to You.
With steps barely a whisper, I
crawl.

The ground quakes,
Disintegrating into a million pieces.
My mind spins frantically,
Moulding shoulders into existence.
Discarding without a
thought-precious promises,
You heart speaks to mine, reminding
me who You are:
"Close your eyes and walk by faith,"
You say.

You are my place of rest.
Inside of You I am secure,
Enclosed and shielded from the sun.
Wrapped in the palm of Your hand,
My eyes look afar off and all I see
Are men given in exchange for me.
I will rest in hope,
Quietly trusting in You.

REST

Come to Me all who are
weary and heavy laden
and I will give you rest.

Come to Me with everything,
Hand over every burden.
Drop the thoughts that weigh you down.
There's no striving in grace.

I am Yours and you are Mine.
I am Yours and you are Mine.
I am Yours and you are Mine.

In quietness and confidence
shall be your strength.
Be still. Be quiet. Lean in.
Rest. I am here. I am near.

Closer than your mind can fathom.
Draw near to Me and
I will draw near to you.

BE STILL AND KNOW THAT I AM GOD

There's no striving in grace.

THE BREVITY OF LIFE

What is life if not lived
in the service of God?

What is breath if not
breathed for His glory?

A passing shadow.
A fleeting mist.
A withering plant.

May I be courageous,
May I be bold,
May I be unrelenting,
May I defy the odds,
To the glory and praise,
Of the One
To whom I shall return.

"The love of God is not created— it is His nature."
—Oswald Chambers

part six

SOME DAYS

Some days, the loneliness will knock the
wind out of your sails.
You'll feel like giving up,
You'll wonder about the apparent
foolishness of waiting for
what you cannot see.

But what is apparent is
often different from what is true.
You will come to the end of yourself,
Your own strength will become weak.

But somehow,
your hope will be restored,
Your heart will be stirred afresh.
Your grip will become stronger.
Your feet will stand firmer.
Because you know
faithful is He who has called you,

He also will do it.

CONVERSATIONS WITH MY FATHER

Dear Child,
I love you on your good days as much as I
do the bad ones,
my trip to Calvary covered it all.

Dear Abba,
my hormones are raging
and everything in me is screaming
gratification,
I never thought I would be on this page
again,
in a different journal
with yet another male specimen.
How was I to know that
time spent in the back of a car
with a preacher was not a sermon?

Dear Child,
the nagging feeling at the back of your
mind
was my way of telling you to wait.
You wanted to, but you were not firm.
You have to learn to mean what you say
just like I taught you to.

Dear Abba,
I'm such an emotional wreck inside,
like pieces of a porcelain doll
carefully glued together.
I wear masks, of different shapes and shades,
whatever suits my audience.
I know you see it all.

Dear Child,
forgive yourself, and forgive him.
Like I forgave you, the alternative is
a downward spiral to perdition.
You do not want to be the reason
why people look back at
Sodom.
Look upon
Calvary and
draw your
strength.
You are stronger
than you think,
and you control your feelings,
they do not control you.

Dear Abba,
what if I fail?
What if I'm not strong enough?
What if I'm a weakling?

Dear Child,
before you were formed in your mother's womb,
I knew you
I chose you before the foundations of the world.
I knew you then, and I chose to love you.
Keep your heart in sync with mine
until you become the masterpiece I already see.

Dear Abba,
sometimes I think your expectations
of me are too high.
Your standard too high to truly attain.
How did your Son do it?
How did He keep Himself
unblemished from the
world?
How did he
resist the
allure of this
world?

Dear Child,
Trust me to keep you from
falling,
Know that my
grace is
sufficient for you.
Abide in me, and I will abide in you.
My yoke is easy and my burden is light.

Dear Abba,
your love is never-ending, overwhelming.
It overflows the river banks.
Its depth is unfathomable.
Its height immeasurable.
I long to know it and
fully understand the depths of it.
Show me.

Dear Child,
I gave my Son in exchange for your life;
so that you could stand before me
with confidence.
Look to Calvary with eyes that see,
then you will know,
I LOVE YOU, CHILD

AUDIENCE OF ONE

I'm a dancer,
dancing to a tune the world
cannot hear.

A heavenly sound,
a glorious symphony.

I'm dancing as My Father sings,
He sits in the audience,
head bobbing in assent.
Or signalling a correction.

As I move to the words.
No one else sits with Him,
He is my audience of one.

JAR OF CLAY

From dust to life—
Your breath made the difference;
from despair to hope,
Your love changed everything.
From a lump of clay to a vessel,
Your hands are moulding me.

I'm a jar of clay,
moulded by Your hands.
Revived by Your breath,
equipped by Your Spirit,
empowered by Your word,
to conquer territories.

Keep me close to Your heart,
may I never forget how much I need You.
May my thirst remind me to drink,
may I be ever renewed.
Ever panting,
ever following,
ever trusting,
like a lamb to its shepherd,
and a daughter to her father.

A PSALM

With You,
my time is redeemed.
Your words upon my heart
strengthen me.
I know that in You,
my peace is inexplicable.
And the joy that brings
is everlasting.

O Lord my God,
You alone will I serve
for the rest of my days.

There is no life
without You,
no hope, no light.

You pick at the strings
of my heart as I make
melodies to You.

I choose You,
today,
always,
forever.

My source, my all.

"There are far, far better things ahead than any we leave behind."

—C.S. Lewis

part seven

LOOKING AHEAD

Yesterday was the day your life changed.
When the house of cards you built on
loftily crafted plans came crashing down.
Buried deep within the rubble of
despair are your hopes and dreams.
Your trust flickers with each pang
of sorrow
as the darkness looms.

The pain will last for a night,
but joy comes with the dawn of a
new day.
Perhaps like Jesus, you are here to
learn obedience.
Or like Sarah, patience.

Tilt your chin upwards,
unveil your eyes.
Let the scales fall.
Look! See the place that I have been
preparing for you.
Do not look to the left or to the right.
For what lies ahead is more glorious than
what has passed.

Before you are jars of grace

Can you see them?
Cast your burdens
upon My shoulders
and draw your
strength for
tomorrow.

My plans for you are
bigger than your
narrow field of
vision can see.
Look ahead child,
and
Stand like Daniel,
Obey like Noah,
Fight like Joshua,
Trust like Abraham.

Daybreak is coming.
Its light will pierce the darkness.
Be still and know that I Am.
For soon, you shall laugh!

LOVE GARDEN

It's springtime.
The season of roses has come.

But what is that I see blossoming
in your garden, my love?
Is not your garden overrun with
poison ivy rooted in offence?

It's springtime.
The season of roses has come.
Would you rather harvest poison or
love?
Tear out the roots now, my darling.
Before they ruin the whole garden.

It's harvest season.
Your real enemy is hiding behind the
shadows,
Playing hide and seek.
Don't be fooled by his tricks.

"The light shines in the darkness, and the darkness can never extinguish it."

—John 1:5 NLT

part eight

LIGHT BE.

Let there be,
And there was — light.
The light shines in the dark,
The darkness cannot invade,
Understand,
Extinguish The light.

Arise, shine.
Let the light in you, be

Awake O sleepers,
The nations await you.
Be awake,
Be alert,
Be present,
Be light.

Creation groans,
The nations moan,
Awake sleeping soldier,

Let the light in you; be.

THIS IS WAR

The battle line is already drawn,
Soldiers are falling in line.
Troops are gathering strength.
The army is getting ready.
Every hand is strong,
Preparing their weapons of warfare.

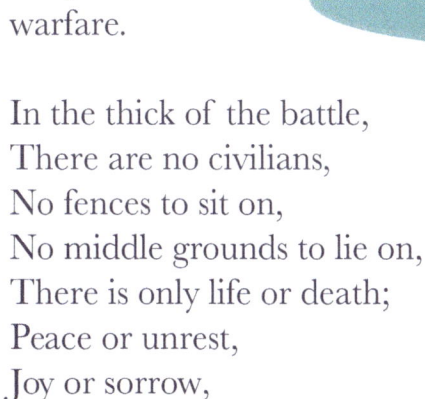

In the thick of the battle,
There are no civilians,
No fences to sit on,
No middle grounds to lie on,
There is only life or death;
Peace or unrest,
Joy or sorrow,

This is war.
Whose side are you on?
And to whom do you belong?
Midnight is coming,
And so is the King of kings.
He is the reward of the righteous
And the Saviour of the lost.
Join His army and live.

KING OF THE JEWS

It was a lonely road to the cross,
Amidst the jeering of enemies
and the tears of friends.
Some called him a fool,
Others called him the King of the Jews.
He was dogged in His pursuit,
Stopping only to catch a breath.

He took upon Himself the sins of the world
So that we all could be called the children of God.
Made right with Him through the blood of His Son, Jesus.

The Great I Am.
Became a man because of us.
His love a mystery we will never be able to
Completely unravel on this side of eternity.

He stands at the door of your heart,
Knocking and gently asking,
"Can I come in?"
I hope your answer will be 'yes'.
The days and nights are going by so fast,
Each leading us closer to the Day of the Lord.
Glory, Glory, Hallelujah.

THE RISING

I see oil
trickling down,
like droplets of rain
in a storm arising.

I see Him—Potter,
moulding the clay to His will,
drawing the hearts of fathers to himself,
finding the lost and healing the broken.

I see fire
spreading relentlessly
through the hearts of men
like dry leaves in harmattan.

I see the eyes of sons light up with knowledge
as the daughters worship recklessly.
I hear angels sing in adoration
as grace flows from the Mercy Seat.

I see Jesus rise with healing in His wings
as the earth and heavens fold,
sin and death cower in defeat
as soldiers are called into battle.

I see the waves crash
as the deafening roar of His voice
thunders through the air
like the sound of many waters.

"Every renaissance comes to the world with a cry; the cry for the human spirit to be free."

—Anne Sullivan

part nine

MAMA'S HOPE

I have heard that Mama used to be great,
She was happy and in love.
Made of wishful thinking and empty promises.
Like fairy tales spun in the wind.
Lost now in the sands of time.

She sits now on the precipice of sanity,
Counting the days until she can truly be free.
Her face lights up as she walks
down the lane paved with
Memories of a time when life was good.
The illusion of her freedom a fleeting reality.

How long has it been,
Since her roads became death-traps?
How long has it been,
Since bomb blasts became a cliché?
How long has it been,
Since her currency delved
headlong into quicksand?

Her heart beats wildly
As she watches in anticipation.
For the emergence of her messiah.
Dark shadows flicker across her horizon.
But still, she keeps the light in view,
Fuelled by the power of her hope.

She asks earnestly in agony,
When will freedom be free?
When will war be at peace?
As she stares into the darkness,
Perhaps like me, she can see Hope
Riding on the wings of tomorrow.

A NATION BLEEDS

Her people groan.
Heads bowed.
Knees aground.

Her cries for help are not in vain,
But she despairs too easily.
Forgetting the victories of years gone by.

If it was not the Lord who has been on her side?
She would have been desolate, and empty
Begging for the crumbs of foreign nations.

Would she hope again
In the valley of the shadow of death?
Would she remain strong and resolute
in the face of Goliath?

The reign of darkness and terror
Is coming to an end.
Light is coming:
Behold, joy comes with it!

National Awakening

The giant is awakening,
Rousing from a sleep so deep.
Everyone thought she was dead.

Like the rainbow before a storm is a promise,
So is the cry of my generation.
A generation that has had enough.

Enough of the tales of when Nigeria was great.
We want to live it too.
"No more," we say "save your tales for another day."
Our time has come.
Our time is now.

ONE DAY SOON

One day soon, our pens will no longer be melancholic, hoping for change.
Soon our ink will dance on paper, happy that the days we longed for are here.

Those who profited from a sad
narrative; a tale of woes
will search for the words to
describe the joy on our
children's faces.

They will sit before blank sheets
and black pens,
praying for the words to
describe our new streets of
gold.

One day soon, our pens will no
longer be melancholic, hoping
for change.
Soon our ink will dance on
paper, happy that the days we
longed for are here.

AUTHOR'S NOTES

"Echoes of Heaven" is in some ways a glimpse into my own journey with God. I have experienced His love and grace at every point in my life; at times when I got weary and felt like giving up, in moments of struggle with sin and self, and in 'dry' seasons when all I needed was a little more of Him.

I can boldly say that submitting my life to the Lordship of Jesus Christ is the best decision I have ever made.

Everything that has happened in my life since then has been coloured by the reality of my identity as a child of God, and my creativity is a huge part of that.

My desire for you, dear reader, is that you will find yourself somewhere in this book and begin your own journey with God or continue from where you are with Him.

I hope that you will know the love of God and experience it for yourself, just as I have.

All my love,

Olamide Oti-Akappo
November, 2022
Ibadan Nigeria

ACKNOWLEDGEMENTS

I am grateful for my parents and siblings who have supported me since day one, and made me believe I could be so much more.

To my amazing friends who have cheered me on since my early days of blogging, the seeds of your encouragement have yielded fruit, thank you.

To my best friend and husband, thank you for being my number-one cheerleader. Thank you for praying this book into existence, and thank you for constantly pushing and encouraging me to write. I love you.

I also want to thank the entire Householder Publishing team for believing in this work enough to take the risk.

God bless you all.